speaking without hesitation

Rhymes, discussions, role play and more

For ages
3-5

Brenda Whittle and Heidi Jayne

Authors
Brenda Whittle and Heidi Jayne

Development Editor
Simret Brar

Editor
Roanne Charles

Assistant Editor
Alex Albrighton

Series Designer
Anna Oliwa

Designer
Geraldine Reidy

Cover Illustration
Craig Cameron/Art Collection

Illustrations
Gaynor Berry

Text © 2008, Brenda Whittle and Heidi Jayne
© 2008 Scholastic Ltd

Designed using Adobe InDesign

Published by Scholastic Ltd
Villiers House
Clarendon Avenue
Leamington Spa
Warwickshire
CV32 5PR

www.scholastic.co.uk

Printed by Bell & Bain

1 2 3 4 5 6 7 8 9   8 9 0 1 2 3 4 5 6 7

British Library Cataloguing-in-Publication Data
A catalogue record for this book is available from the British Library.

ISBN 978-0439-94557-8

Acknowledgements

The publishers gratefully acknowledge permission to reproduce the following copyright material:

Wes Magee for the use of 'Stroke the Cat' by Wes Magee from *Stroke the Cat* by Wes Magee © 2005, Wes Magee (2005, QED).

Brenda Williams for the use of 'Shoes' by Brenda Williams from *Themes for Early Years: Clothes* by Anne Piper © 1998, Brenda Williams (1998, Scholastic Ltd).

Her Majesty's Stationery Office for the use of extracts from *Practice Guidance for the Early Years Foundation Stage* © Crown copyright, reproduced under the terms of the Click-Use Licence.

Every effort has been made to trace copyright holders for the works reproduced in this book, and the publishers apologise for any inadvertent omissions.

Contents

Introduction

Speaking without hesitation

Speaking without hesitation is one of a series of books containing 'outside the box' ideas for practitioners working with children in the early years. Children's interests and joy for life form the basis for the activities in this series. The activities build on children's natural instincts to be doing, investigating, making, creating and solving problems. They are designed to excite and stimulate children as they learn through using their senses, being active and thinking for themselves.

But why speaking without hesitation?

In a world of countless television channels, computer games and background noise, children can become passive listeners, not needing to react to or talk about what they see or hear. The activities in this book have been developed to excite children into reacting spontaneously with enjoyment and enthusiasm to what they hear, see, smell, taste and touch; to encourage confident interaction with others and the use of language for many different purposes. In

order to include reticent speakers and restless listeners, activities need to grab the children's attention, and the atmosphere in the setting needs to be supportive, friendly and relaxed, where children can be confident that they will be listened to and their contributions will be valued.

Wanting to speak and listen

The activities in this book provide children with compelling reasons to want to talk, listen and communicate with others as they use their senses to explore the world around them and delight in the richness and rhythm of language in stories, songs and rhymes.

How to use this book

The book is in three sections:

● Chapter 1: 'Language for communication' introduces children to the joys of listening to and using language to communicate with each other and adults in a wide range of appealing situations. These include enjoying the fun of a role-play fair, sharing thoughts and empathising with story

characters, and feeling the wind and questioning what it is and where it comes from.

● Chapter 2: 'Language for thinking' includes a wide range of activities to inspire children to talk, interact and collaborate as they make sense of the world around them. They are encouraged to reflect and talk about past experiences and feelings, including during imaginative play and role play. They predict what will happen when they add different substances to water, make observations as they dig holes and use imagination and creativity when presented with boxes and drapes.

● Chapter 3: 'Messages and clues' challenges children to discuss and decide together what to do next when they find clues and messages in a variety of forms. They find a pirate's message in a bottle in the water tray, a taped message from an octopus whose babies are playing hide and seek (based on the poem, 'Octopus' in *Commotion in the Ocean* by Giles Andreae) and work out who is coming for breakfast from the clues on the table.

The activities

Planning and learning objectives

Links to the Development Matters objectives and Early Learning Goals for Communication, language and literacy (CLL) in the DfES document *Practice Guidance for The Early Years Foundation Stage* are shown for each activity to aid planning. The

activities are all cross-curricu.... main link to one of the other Learning and Development is uiso snown where appropriate.

Support and extension

Each activity has suggestions for how it may be adapted or extended according to children's needs and stage of development.

Assessment

Practitioners can assess children against the Development Matters objectives shown for each activity. Most of the activities are designed for small groups, enabling practitioners to observe individual children's progress and to aid assessment to inform future planning.

Further activities

These provide more suggestions for developing lively ideas linked to the main activity.

Play links

Ideas for play-learning linked to the main activity are given to continue the theme into other Areas of Learning and Development, such as opportunities for investigations or role play.

Home links

In order to promote and foster a partnership with parents and carers for the benefit of the children, a suggestion is given in each activity to link the learning in the setting with that in the home.

Health and safety

Follow the health and safety guidelines in place for your particular setting or local authority.

Abbreviations

References to Areas of Learning and Development in the DfES document *The Early Years Foundation Stage: Practice Guidance:*

● Personal social and emotional development **(PSED)**

● Communication, language and literacy **(CLL)**

● Problem solving, reasoning and numeracy **(PSRN)**

● Knowledge and understanding of the world **(KUW)**

● Physical development **(PD)**

● Creative development **(CD)**

Language for communication

Stroke the cat

Children have fun playing with a realistic toy cat in its basket as they join in with the refrain and actions in Wes Magee's rhythmic poem, 'Stroke the Cat'.

What you need

A small cat basket or cardboard box containing: blanket, realistic toy cat, plastic food and water bowls, plastic bottle labelled *water*, plastic container labelled *food*, soft brush; the poem 'Stroke the Cat' on photocopiable page 7 on laminated card.

Learning objectives
Language for Communication
● Join in with repeated refrains and anticipate key events and phrases in rhymes and stories. **(CLL)**
Early Learning Goals
● Enjoy listening to and using spoken and written language, and readily turn to it in their play and learning. **(CLL)**

What to do

● Show the children the cat in the basket. Encourage them to touch and talk about it, commenting on whether or not it is real, what it feels like and looks like. Encourage talk about cats the children may have as pets. Identify the different parts of the cat's body, including paws and whiskers.

● Talk about the things a cat needs to keep it healthy, such as food, water and somewhere comfortable to sleep. Read together the labels on the water and food containers. Model pouring water and food into the appropriate bowls and brushing the cat's fur.

● Recite 'Stroke the Cat' by Wes Magee, using the appropriate actions as you do so (stroke, lift, shake hands and so on). Repeat the poem, encouraging the children to hear the rhythm of the words and join in with the refrain and actions, anticipating what will come next. Read the poem together, encouraging the children to use the illustrations as cues.

Support and extension

● Support younger children as they say the refrain with you.
● Ask older children to listen for the initial sound in the word *cat* and to find and point to the letter *c* on the poem card.

Further activities

● Share other poems and stories about cats, such as 'Pussy cat, pussy cat where have you been?', *Cats Sleep Anywhere* by Eleanor Farjeon, *Ginger* by Charlotte Voake and *A Kitten Called Moonlight* by Martin Waddell.
● Place the cat, basket and equipment on a blanket outdoors, along with picture books and non-fiction books about cats, to encourage play, reading and talk.

Home link

Encourage the children to look out for and talk to their parents or carers about cats they see near where they live and on their way to the setting.

Cross-curricular links
Exploration and Investigation
● Show curiosity and interest in the features of objects and living things. **(KUW)**
Early Learning Goal
● Find out about, and identify, some features of living things, objects and events they observe. **(KUW)**

Stroke the Cat

Stroke the cat,
stroke the cat
and lift it from the floor.

Stroke the cat,
stroke the cat
and shake hands with its paw.

Stroke the cat,
stroke the cat
and scratch its head once more.

Stroke the cat,
stroke the cat
– then shoo it through the door!

Wes Magee

A very special day

The children are invited to bring in an object that has special significance for them. To encourage them to tell others about it they sit in a special chair covered in drapes and stars.

Early communicators begin to gain confidence when speaking in a small group, with adult support.
More confident communicators explain to the group what is special about their object and why they have brought it in.

What you need
Photocopies of the invitation on page 10 and certificate on page 11; display area including: chair, display board and table covered in sumptuous fabrics and stars; basket of items special to you, plus some 'spares' for children's use; blank labels and cards; children's digital camera or camcorder; drinks, fruit and biscuits.

What to do
● Write out the invitations.
● To prepare the children for the special day, show them the basket of items that are significant to you. Talk about each item, saying why it is precious, and encouraging comments and questions from the children. Ask the children to think of things that are special to them, for example an outfit or uniform worn for a favourite activity such as

karate or ballet, a swimming badge, a book, a photograph of a much-loved person or pet, or a reminder of a special day such as a postcard or birthday card.
● Explain to the children that you are planning a special day and they are invited to bring in one thing that is important to them. Give the children their invitations to take home.
● On the special day, set up an area to include a chair, table and display board dressed with drapes, swags and stars. When the children arrive with their special things, encourage them to label their own items or ask an adult to help them. Keep a few special objects to hand in case some children are unable to bring anything.
● Gather a small group at a time in the special area and ask if anyone would like to tell the group about

Learning objectives
Language for Communication
● Have confidence to speak to others about their own wants and interests. **(CLL)**
Early Learning Goal
● Interact with others, negotiating plans and activities and taking turns in conversation. **(CLL)**

their object. More confident children may choose to sit in the special chair as they talk. Invite the children to describe, explain and perhaps give instructions about how to use their object. Support the speaker and involve the other children by making comments and asking questions. For example:

- *You've done very well to get your swimming badge Mia. Who else likes to go swimming?*
- *I love Toby's photo of him playing football. Shall we make a special area outside just for football?*

● Throughout the day, and as long as you have permission, help the children to make a record of their special objects or themselves sitting in the special chair, using a simple digital camera or camcorder. Note down comments to write on cards for adding to the display: *Mia brought her swimming badge. Toby likes playing football.*

● End the day with a special tea party of drinks, biscuits and pieces of fruit. Complete the certificates for the children to take home.

Support and extension

● Support younger children by asking simple questions about their special object.
● Ask older children more open-ended questions and help to extend their vocabulary during the discussions.

Further activities

● Choose one or two items from the display as a starting point for other activities. For example, practise playing football together, share a special story book or search the internet for pictures of pets.

● Set up a drawing area with paper, pencils and crayons to encourage children to make pictures of their special things. Display the drawings in a special book to share.

Play link

Make an impromptu 'special things' corner with cushions to sit on and a box containing a selection of unusual, eye-catching or tactile objects, such as beautiful shells, a necklace, attractive pictures, patterned and textured fabric, conkers and driftwood. **(KUW)**

Home link

Invite parents and carers to come to the end of the session and share the display of special things with their children.

Cross-curricular links
ICT
● Know how to operate simple equipment. **(KUW)**
Early Learning Goal
● Find out about and identify the uses of everyday technology and use information and communication technology and programmable toys to support their learning. **(KUW)**

A very special day – invitation

A Very Special Day

To _____

On _____

we will be having a Very Special Day.

Please bring something that is special to you, such as a birthday card, photograph, swimming badge, book or dance shoes.

A Very Special Day

Name _____

My special object is _____

It is special to me because _____

_____

Speaking without hesitation

www.scholastic.co.uk

A very special day – certificate

Certificate

Well done, _____:

Today was our Very Special Day at _____

_____

and you talked about _____

_____

Signed _____

Date _____

Speaking without hesitation

SCHOLASTIC
www.scholastic.co.uk

In the park

In this activity, the children are enticed to come and listen when they hear others talking about a quirky picture showing a day in the park.

What you need

An A3 photocopy on stiff paper of the picture on page 13.

What to do

● Gather a group of two or three children around you and show them the picture. Begin by making your own observations and asking questions to gain the children's attention, such as:

● *Look, the children are in the park. Do you think it is a hot day? How can you tell?*

● *What are those cats doing?*

● *Is that a baby in the buggy?*

Early communicators listen to comments about the picture and begin to contribute their own comments.
More confident communicators listen attentively to others' comments, respond and ask questions.

● Encourage the children to talk about and enjoy the things they see in the picture. Keep the attention of reluctant listeners by your comments and questions. Gradually induce all of the children into talking and listening, responding to each other's comments and observations. Model ways to do this with supportive comments such as:

● *James said the doll looks as though she is going to fall off the swing. I think he's right. Look, she's only holding on with one hand.*

● *Sevita said those sandwiches are making her feel hungry – they are making me hungry too!*

Make sure the comments and observations are kept lively and interesting to 'draw in' children so that they are fascinated and want to listen.

Support and extension

● Support reluctant listeners by including them in your questions and showing that you value their responses.

● Encourage children who listen attentively to take turns in responding and asking questions.

Further activity

Tell the children that you want them to look carefully at the picture and help you to make a similar 'picture' in the setting, using real items. Assemble a slide, climbing equipment and the other props needed, such as teddy bears, dolls and picnic items. Invite the children to set the scene, talking about what they are doing and listening to others' opinions about the things they need and where they should be placed. When everything is ready, help the children to take photographs of the scene and enjoy playing inside the 'picture'. Display the photographs and original picture as talking points.

Home link

Invite the children to show their parents or carers the picture and photographs, explaining what they have been doing.

Learning objectives
Language for Communication
● Listen to others in one-to-one or small groups when conversation interests them. **(CLL)**
Early Learning Goal
● Sustain attentive listening, responding to what they have heard with relevant comments, questions or actions. **(CLL)**

Cross-curricular links
Dispositions and Attitudes
Have a positive approach to activities and events. **(PSED)**
Early Learning Goal
Continue to be interested, excited and motivated to learn. **(PSED)**

In the park

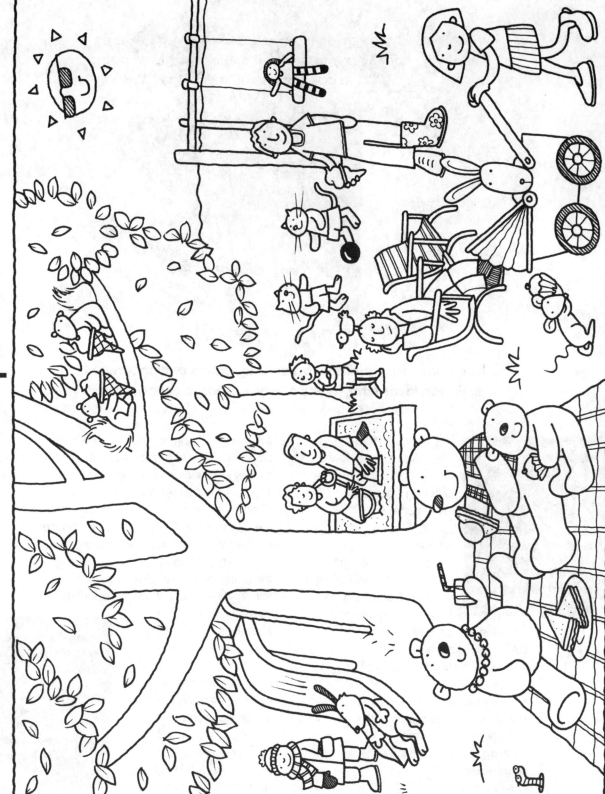

SCHOLASTIC
www.scholastic.co.uk

Walking, walking

The children enjoy a simple action song before putting forward their own ideas for a variety of new actions to choose from.

Early communicators begin to contribute their ideas in a small group and listen to other children's comments.
More confident communicators put forward their ideas, take turns in conversation and take notice of other children's contributions.

What you need
The song/rhyme below written on a board or large sheet of paper; paper; thick felt-tipped pen.

What to do
● Arrange a small group of children in a circle, facing inwards. Teach them the song 'Walking, walking', sung to the tune of 'Frère Jacques':

Walking, walking,
Walking, walking. *(Children walk on the spot)*
Hop, hop, hop,
Hop, hop, hop *(Children hop on the spot)*
Running, running, running,
Running, running, running. *(Children run on the spot)*
Now we stop.
Now we stop. *(Children stop)*

● Repeat the song and actions and then ask the children to move around the room as they sing and do the actions again.
● Gather the children together in a circle, to sit down and rest. Tell them that you want them to think for a minute or two to choose a different action to replace walking, such as jumping, crawling or rolling, and to tell the group their ideas. Give the children thinking time and then ask for volunteers to make their suggestions. Model attentive listening, and make supportive comments, talking about the children's different ideas. Make a note of the suggestions and who made them. Ensure that the children understand the importance of taking turns and listening to each other's ideas.

Learning objectives
Language for Communication
● Initiate conversation, attend to and take account of what others say. **(CLL)**
Early Learning Goal
● Interact with others, negotiating plans and activities and taking turns in conversation. **(CLL)**

● Sing the song and perform the actions again, this time changing the first line and crediting the child who made the suggestion. For example, *Let's use Emily's idea, 'Jumping, jumping…'* or *Andrew said, 'Creeping, creeping…'*

● When the children are resting later, read together the words for the song, pointing out the repeated words and rhymes. Tell the children that you want their help to change two actions in the song (the first and third lines), replacing them with their own action words. Encourage children to put forward their ideas, listen to and comment on each other's suggestions. When you have decided together on the new words, write them on a large sheet of paper for the children to read and refer to later.

Support and extension
● Support and encourage younger children so that they have the confidence to put forward their own ideas and comments in a group situation.

● Challenge older children to work with a friend, trying out different movements to use in the song, and then telling the group together about their ideas.

Further activities
● Provide each child with streamers or ribbons to hold. Play different kinds of dance music and ask the children to move in different ways as they respond to the music. Take the opportunity to extend the children's movement vocabulary, introducing words such as *turning, skipping, gliding, swirling, twirling, whirling* and *shaking*.

● Give children time to be 'in charge' and gain confidence by playing 'Follow my leader'. Lead a line of children through the setting or outside, asking them to copy your movements. Ask children to wave when they have an idea for a different movement and choose a child to come to the front and take a turn at being the leader.

Play link
Provide dance music, a music player and a box of percussion instruments outside to encourage children to respond freely to music through movement and use of the instruments. **(CD)**

Home link
Suggest that parents and carers encourage their children to experiment in moving in lots of different ways when at home in the garden or walking in the park.

Cross-curricular links
Making Relationships
● Feel safe and secure, and show a sense of trust. **(PSED)**
Early Learning Goal
● Work as part of a group or class, taking turns and sharing fairly, understanding that there need to be agreed values and codes of behaviour for groups of people, including adults and children, to work together harmoniously. **(PSED)**

Sandcastles

The children enter a competition in sandcastle building and explain what they have been doing to a 'reporter' from the local radio station.

Early communicators talk about what they are doing as they make their sandcastles.
More confident communicators use simple mathematical language to explain how they built their sandcastles.

What you need

A large sand tray or sandpit (ideally, large enough for the children to stand inside) filled with damp sand; buckets of dry sand; small suitcase containing sun hats, sunglasses and T-shirts; jugs and watering cans; water; assorted shapes and sizes of buckets, yoghurt pots and other plastic containers; spades; rakes; flags; shells; voice recorder and player; timer with alarm/bell; prize stickers; 'reporter'/press badge.

What to do

● Tell the children that today they are going to pretend they are on holiday at the seaside and will be taking part in a competition to build the best sandcastle on the beach. Invite them to choose items from the suitcase to wear.
● Ask the children to touch the dry sand and then the damp sand, comparing the feel of them. Ask the children to dip their hands in water and then take a handful of dry sand. When they open their hands and let go of the sand, what happens to their hands? Does all of the sand fall off? Now, with dry hands, ask them to see if they can shape the dry sand. What happens?
● Demonstrate how to make the base of a sandcastle, piling up damp sand and shaping it, patting it with a spade and making lines in it with a rake. Then add individual towers and other castles using the buckets or containers, and decorate them with flags and shells. Model talk and observations about the shapes and differences in size between the sandcastles.
● Tell the children that when the competition starts

you will set the timer, and the competition will finish when the timer rings. Explain that you will be pretending to be a reporter from a local radio show who will watch them make their sandcastles and ask them questions when they have finished. Wear a large badge saying, *Reporter*.
● When the competition has finished, introduce yourself as the reporter, recording your voice as you do so. Play back the recording to the children and explain that you want them to tell you about their sandcastles while you record their voices. Play back the recordings and congratulate the children. Either choose a winner or award stickers to each child.

Support and extension
● Work alongside younger children as they make their sandcastles, asking questions and encouraging them to talk about shape and size.
● Encourage older children to use mathematical language to describe the shapes of their sandcastles when they are being interviewed.

Further activities
● Use a sandpit or pile play sand onto a large ground sheet outside. Encourage the children to work collaboratively to make one large sandcastle between them, talking, negotiating and explaining as they work.

Check that you have permission to film the children before using a camcorder to record the building and talking in progress. Watch the recording later with the children and talk about what they did.
● Make an ice castle. Choose a large plastic bowl to make the 'castle' and yoghurt pots, egg cups or jelly moulds to make shapes to go on top or around the castle. Fill the containers with water and leave to freeze. Do not let children handle ice straight from the freezer. As the children remove the ice from the containers and assemble the castle, encourage them to talk about the feel of the ice and to explain what they are doing. Compare making the ice castle with making the sandcastle.

Play link
Provide yellow and orange construction bricks, straws, paper rectangles and triangles, sticky tape, scissors and felt-tipped pens. Challenge the children to make 'sandcastles' and decorate them with their own flags. **(PD)**

Home link
Ask the children to explain to their parents or carers how they built their sandcastles.

Cross-curricular links
Shape, Space and Measures
● Show interest in shape by sustained construction activity or by talking about shapes or arrangements. **(PSRN)**
Early Learning Goal
● Use language such as circle or bigger to describe the shape and size of solids and flat shapes. **(PSRN)**

In my toybox

Children enjoy and talk about Mick Inkpen's story
Kipper's Toybox **before bringing in their own favourite toys to talk about.**

What you need
Kipper's Toybox by Mick Inkpen (1995, Hodder Children's Books); a cardboard box with a hole in one corner, containing assorted toys in varying condition; whiteboard or large sheet of paper; photocopiable page 19. Ask the children to bring in a toy from home that they especially like. Emphasise that it should be a favourite toy, not the best or most expensive. Ideally, it will be a different item from that chosen for 'A very special day'. If a child is unable to bring in a toy, let them choose one from around the setting.

What to do
● Read *Kipper's Toybox*. Talk about the story, the toys that Kipper had in the box and the hole in the box made by the mice.
● Show the children the toybox you have prepared. Ask them who they think could have made the hole in your box. Now look at each toy item in turn, encouraging the children to talk about the toys' appearance and how they would be played with.
● Create a relaxed atmosphere, for example sitting together with the favourite toys in a quiet corner on a blanket, inside or outside. Ask the children to bring their chosen toys. Encourage the children to talk about their toys, saying where they came

> **Early communicators** begin to talk about their own special toys.
> **More confident communicators** learn and use new words associated with their toys.

from, and when and how they play with them. Help to extend their vocabulary through questions and comments:
● *What does your teddy bear feel like? Is he hard or squashy?*
● *What is your shiny car made of?*
● *Your doll's face feels smooth. What does her hair feel like?*
● Write some of the key words on the whiteboard or paper and read them together.

Support and extension
● Encourage younger children with precise questions as they describe their toys.
● Let older children talk about their toys to the group, and help them to extend their vocabulary by introducing new words.

Further activity
Help each child to take a photograph of their toy using a digital camera. Make the photographs into a slide show to watch on screen. Also help the children to print their photographs and glue them into their own toybox on photocopiable page 19.

Home link
Encourage the children to bring in a favourite toy.

> **Learning objectives**
> **Language for Communication**
> ● Use vocabulary focused on objects and people that are of particular importance to them. **(CLL)**
> **Early Learning Goal**
> ● Extend their vocabulary, exploring the meanings and sounds of new words. **(CLL)**

> **Cross-curricular links**
> **ICT**
> ● Know how to operate simple equipment. **(KUW)**
> **Early Learning Goal**
> ● Find out about and identify the uses of everyday technology and use information and communication technology and programmable toys to support their learning. **(KUW)**

In my toybox

Fold

Speaking without hesitation

Fun at the fair

The children help to make simple fairground games. Then they listen and respond to instructions on how to play the games.

What you need

Large cardboard boxes; plastic or cardboard tubes; cartridge paper; string; garden canes; stapler; paints and brushes; balls of different sizes, beanbags, quoits and skittles; plastic ducks; a small football net; a fishing net; bricks and blocks; cones; buckets/bowls; ride-on toys; sand timer.

What to do

● Ask the children if they have ever been to a fair. Talk about the things people might do at a fair and tell the children that they are going to help you make a fair that they can all enjoy. Explain that they will be trying things such as throwing, catching, riding bikes and knocking over skittles.
● Choose a bright colour scheme for the fair, such as red and yellow. Cut the cartridge paper into rectangles and triangles for flags and bunting. Involve the children in painting the cardboard boxes, flags and bunting triangles in stripes or other patterns. When dry, glue or staple the flags to pieces of garden cane and fold one side of the paper triangles over a length of string and staple in place to make the bunting.
● Work together to set up the play activities that could include:
  ● Throwing beanbags into a bucket.
  ● Building a tower of bricks on an upturned box.
  ● Dropping balls into a cardboard tube.
  ● Throwing balls to knock over skittles.
  ● Kicking a ball into a net.
  ● Fishing ducks out of a shallow bowl of water. (Closely supervise all water activities.)
  ● A 'roundabout' made by using cones to make a big circle and arranging ride-on toys around the edge of it.

● Put up the flags and lengths of bunting around the area, ensuring they do not cause a safety hazard.

● When the fair is ready to open, gather the children together and tell them that they must listen carefully. Talk through and demonstrate the ways to use the different objects and pieces of equipment. Use all available adults to assist with the activities, giving clear instructions to the children as they take part, checking that they respond appropriately. For example:

  ● *Throw the beanbags into the bucket.*
  ● *Put the bricks on top of the box.*
  ● *Drop the balls into the tube.*
  ● *Ride round and round the edge of the circle.*

Support and extension

● Support younger children by talking part with them and making sure that they listen to and understand the instructions.

● Give older children more than one instruction to follow. For example:

  ● *Start the sand timer and see how many ducks you can catch before the sand runs out.*
  ● *Stand behind the line and kick the ball into the net.*

Further activities

● Take a break from the activities, sit together on a rug and share drinks and snacks. Invite the children to talk about what they have been doing and what they enjoyed most. Ask them to put forward their own ideas for other activities and games they would like to include. Encourage the children to listen carefully to each other's ideas, responding with relevant comments.

● Include the clearing away of the fair as an important listening activity. Gather the children together and give individual children simple, clear instructions, using positional language, for putting away each activity. For example:

  ● *Put all of the bricks in the red box.*
  ● *Put the ducks next to the sink.*
  ● *Put the skittles inside the bag.*
  ● *Put the bikes in front of the shed.*

Play link

Provide a selection of boxes, cardboard tubes, balls, beanbags and quoits for children to use to make their own fairground games. **(PD)**

Home link

Ask parents and carers to talk to their children about their memories of visiting the funfair when they were children.

Cross-curricular links
Using Equipment and Materials
● Use increasing control over an object, such as a ball, by touching, pushing, patting, throwing, catching or kicking it. **(PD)**
Early Learning Goal
● Use a range of small and large equipment. **(PD)**

The snowman

The children enjoy a poem about a snowman. They talk about shapes and sizes when they make snowmen from spheres and cones.

What you need

An A3 photocopy of page 23; balls of different sizes; orange card cones; elastic; Blu-Tack®; play dough; pebbles; coloured paper and card; scissors; carrots (optional).

What to do

● Enjoy reading the poem together two or three times. Encourage the children to join in with the actions and words.

● Ask the children what a snowman looks like. What shapes would they need to make one? Describe the shapes as being a large ball or sphere for the body and a smaller one for the head. If you have snow, let the children make large snowballs and create their own snowmen with carrot noses. Otherwise, ask the children to choose a ball for a snowman's body and one for the head. Talk about the difference in sizes:

● Should the snowman's head be bigger or smaller than his body?

● Which ball is bigger/smaller?

● Stick the larger ball to the table with Blu-Tack®. Fix the smaller ball on top. Say the poem again, then ask what else the snowman needs. Talk about the carrot nose and ask the children to choose a cone of the right size. Secure the cone to the snowman's head with elastic. Ask the children to describe the shape of the cones, using words such as *pointy*.

● Invite the children to make their own snowmen by forming two balls from play dough and adding a cone nose. Provide pebbles, paper and card for eyes, scarf and hat.

Early communicators listen to the poem and join in with the actions. **More confident communicators** listen attentively and draw pictures in response to the poem.

Learning objectives

Language for Communication

● Use language for an increasing range of purposes. **(CLL)**

Early Learning Goal

● Listen with enjoyment and respond to stories songs and other music, rhymes and poems and make up their own stories, songs, rhymes and poems. **(CLL)**

Support and extension

● Talk to younger children about what happens in the poem.

● Encourage older children to illustrate the poem and talk about their pictures.

Further activities

● Take a variety of balls outside and ask the children to listen carefully to your instructions. For example:

  ● *Find a big ball and bounce it.*

  ● *Find a small ball and roll it.*

● Provide some card cones and assorted spun-paper or polystyrene balls. Ask the children to see what happens when they roll the shapes, sort them by size or put cones inside cones or balls inside cones.

Home link

Suggest that the children teach the poem to someone at home.

Cross-curricular links

Shape, Space and Measures

● Begin to use mathematical names for 'solid' 3D shapes and 'flat' 2D shapes, and mathematical terms to describe shapes. **(PSRN)**

Early Learning Goal

● Use language such as *circle* or *bigger* to describe the shape and size of solids and flat shapes. **(PSRN)**

A round little snowman

A round little snowman

Had a carrot nose;
(Point to nose)

Along came a rabbit
(Show hopping movements with hand)

And what do you suppose?

That hungry little bunny,

Looking for his lunch,
(Flat hand above eyes, scanning distance)

ATE the snowman's carrot nose...
(Point to nose)

Nibble, nibble, CRUNCH!
(Munching movement with hand to mouth)

Anon

SCHOLASTIC
www.scholastic.co.uk

March to the beat

After hearing the famous rhyme, the children take on the roles of the grand old Duke of York's men, listen for the beat and march in time to the music.

What you need

A tin of toy soldiers or photocopied and laminated toy soldiers from page 25; marching music; music player.

What to do

● Gather the children in a circle and show them the tin of soldiers. Explain that these soldiers are part of a nursery rhyme. They are very tired because they have been marching up and down a hill. Can the children work out which nursery rhyme it is? When you have established it is 'The Grand old Duke of York', ask the children if they will help the soldiers (the Duke of York's men) by pretending to be them and march up and down while the soldiers have a rest. Explain that they will need to practise marching on the spot first before going outside. Sing the rhyme together, standing tall like soldiers, swinging arms and listening carefully in order to maintain the marching beat.

● When everyone is joining in, march and sing your way outside, pretending to march to the top of a hill, down again and then going only halfway up.

● Gather in a circle to rest, and say that there are many examples of marching music. Play recordings of marches, encouraging the children to listen attentively

Learning objectives
Language for Communication
● Use language for an increasing range of purposes. **(CLL)**
Early Learning Goal
● Listen with enjoyment and respond to stories, songs and other music, rhymes and poems and make up their own stories, songs, rhymes and poems. **(CLL)**

Early communicators
listen to music and become aware of rhythm and a steady beat.
More confident communicators listen and respond to music, enjoying the rhythm and keeping a steady beat.

and clap, tap or stamp in time to the beat.

● Return to the tin of toy soldiers and explain that now they are rested they can join in with more marching. Invite each child to take a soldier and 'march' him up, down and halfway up a hill as you sing the rhyme.

Support and extension

● Help younger children become aware of the steady beat by marching on the spot with them.

● After listening to different marches, ask older children to say which they prefer and why.

Further activity

Talk about the words in the rhyme. The Duke of York had ten thousand men. Is that a lot? Are there ten thousand men in the tin? Count how many toy soldiers there are. Ask the children to draw and cut out more soldiers. How many are there now? Are there too many to count? Place the soldiers in rows of two, five or ten to make them easier to count.

Home link

Give each child a laminated toy soldier to encourage them to sing the nursery rhyme at home.

Cross-curricular links
Creating Music and Dance
● Imitate and create movement in response to music. **(CD)**
Early Learning Goal
● Recognise and explore how sounds can be changed, sing simple songs from memory, recognise repeated sounds and sound patterns and match movements to music. **(CD)**

March to the beat

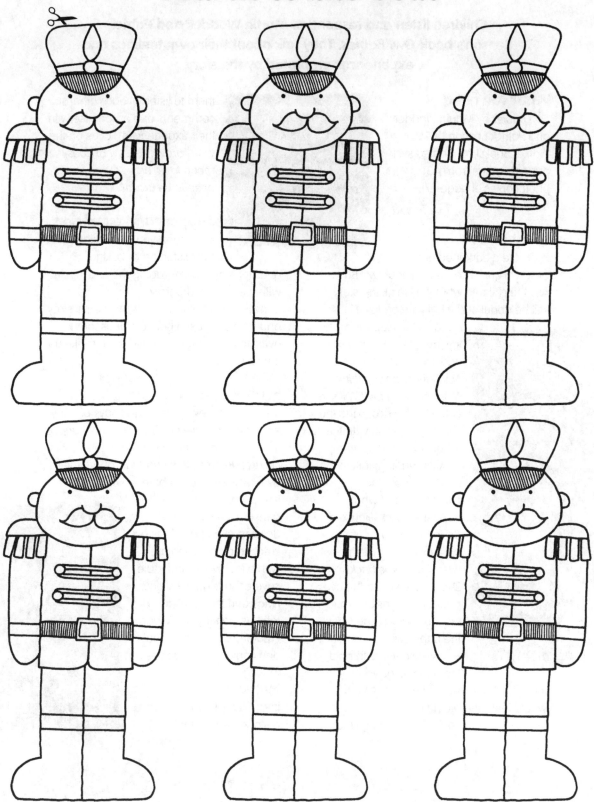

SCHOLASTIC

www.scholastic.co.uk

All alone

Children listen and respond to Martin Waddell and Patrick Benson's book *Owl Babies*. They talk about their own feelings and experiences prompted by the story.

What you need

Owl Babies by Martin Waddell and Patrick Benson (1995, Walker Books); laminated stick puppets made from A3 photocopies of page 27); dowels; torch.

What to do

● Create a darkened area, lit by torchlight. Show the cover of *Owl Babies.* Ask the children what they think the story will be about and what time of day it is.
Read the story, pausing to talk about the illustrations and involve the children. Ask: *Where do you think Mummy has gone? Will she come back?* Encourage the children to join in with the refrain *I want my mummy.*
● After reading, talk to the children about the characters and what happened. Ask: *How did Bill feel when his mummy had gone? How did he feel when she came back?* Show the children the owl puppets and ask them to work out which one is Bill, the baby owl.
● Ask volunteers to hold the puppets as you re-read the story. Invite the children to say how they would feel if they could not find the person who was looking after them. Encourage

> **Early communicators** listen to the story and join in with the repeated phrase.
> **More confident communicators** listen to and retell the story before making up their own stories.

them to listen to each other's comments and empathise with their experiences. Focus on the word *brave.* Ask: *What does it mean to be brave? Do we ever need to be brave?*

Support and extension

● Support younger children in their listening by asking questions and encouraging them to join in with the repeated phrase.
● Invite older children to help retell the story and then suggest other scenarios for the owls, to encourage the children to make up their own stories.

Further activities

● Hold up an owl puppet and say, for example, *This little owl is feeling sad/happy/ frightened because…* Encourage the children to empathise and talk about their own feelings to contribute the rest of the sentence.
● Inspire children to develop their own ideas by creating a darkened area with a low woodland table covered in textured fabric, twigs and leaves. Add torches, soft toy woodland creatures, the owl puppets and copies of *Owl Babies.*

Home link

Invite parents and carers to a storytime session.

> **Learning objectives**
> **Language for Communication**
> ● Listen to stories with increasing attention and recall. **(CLL)**
> ● Describe main story settings, events and principal characters. **(CLL)**
> **Early Learning Goals**
> ● Sustain attentive listening, responding to what they have heard with relevant comments, questions or actions. **(CLL)**
> ● Listen with enjoyment and respond to stories, songs and other music, rhymes and poems and make up their own stories, songs, rhymes and poems. **(CLL)**

> **Cross-curricular links**
> **Self-confidence and Self-esteem**
> ● Express needs and feelings in appropriate ways. **(PSED)**
> **Early Learning Goal**
> ● Have a developing awareness of their own needs, views and feelings, and be sensitive to the needs, views and feelings of others. **(PSED)**

All alone

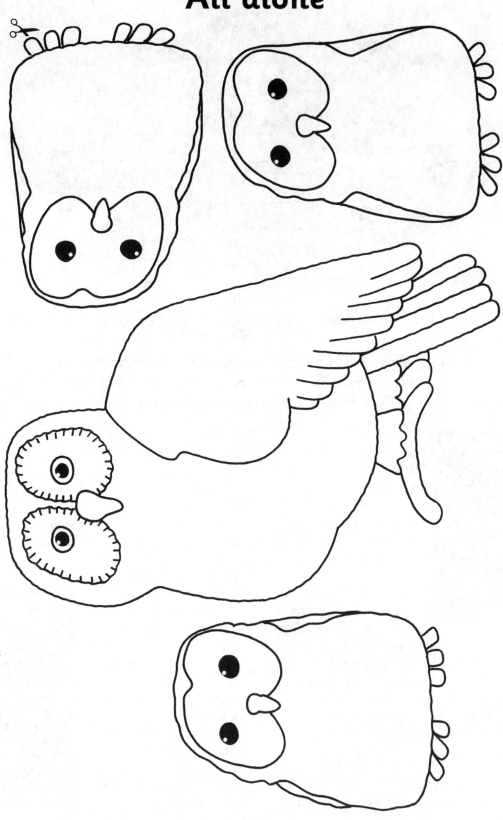

A monster story

Taking inspiration from David McKee's story _Not Now, Bernard,_ the children have fun creating and talking about their own monster and taking it on adventures.

Early communicators listen to the story, join in with the refrain and talk about what happens.
More confident communicators listen attentively to the way the story is read, join in using a different voice for each character and go on to make up their own stories.

What you need
Not Now, Bernard by David McKee (1982, Red Fox); a large cardboard box; scissors; glue; powder paints; large brushes; card; thick black felt-tipped pens; painting aprons.

What to do
● Show the children the book, read the title together and talk about the cover illustration. What do the children think the story will be about? Begin to read the story, using a different voice for each character. Reassure the children that the events of the story are make-believe and would not happen in real life!

● Remind the children to listen very carefully as you re-read the story. Invite them to join in with the refrain _Not now, Bernard_ and the speeches _ROAR_ and _But I'm a monster,_ imitating your tone of voice and different character voices if possible.

● Now tell the children that you want them to make their own monster, similar to the one in the story. Take the cardboard box and cut out a large mouth shape, big enough to allow toys to pass through. Count the monster's fingers and toes from the book illustrations and help the children to draw and cut out large card hands and feet. Tape these to the sides and base of the box. Now count the monster's teeth and horns, make these from card and glue them to the model. Advise the children to refer to the illustrations again to decide which colours to mix to

Learning objectives
Language for Communication
● Listen to stories with increasing attention and recall. **(CLL)**
Early Learning Goal
● Listen with enjoyment and respond to stories, songs and other music, rhymes and poems and make up their own stories, songs, rhymes and poems. **(CLL)**

paint the monster. Help them to experiment with colour mixing until they find the right combination to make purple. Let them use large brushes to paint the monster and, when dry, add yellow horns and nails, and draw in the other features using thick black felt-tipped pens.

● Use the monster as the starting point for making up stories together. For example, you could take the monster into the book corner and create a story about it coming into the setting before the children arrived that morning and eating the books until its tummy was so full it could not eat any more. The children can 'post' the books into the monster's mouth as they use 'monster' voices to tell the story.

Support and extension

● Give younger children time to use the illustrations to aid their understanding as they listen to the story.

● Challenge older children to look for details in the illustrations that are not mentioned in the text, such as Mother spilling the paint or the bandage on Father's finger after he used the hammer.

Further activities

● Take the monster model outside and use whatever props are available to stimulate the children into making up more monster adventures. For example, the monster could eat all of the washing from the line, ride to the seaside on a scooter and eat all the fish in the sea or eat all the animals at the zoo. Check first that you have permission to photograph the children and then take photographs of the monster's adventures and use the pictures as further talking points.

● Use the photographs to remind the children of the monster's adventures and ask them to choose their favourite one to retell as you record their words on tape. Help them to retell the story and then play back the recording for them to listen to and compare the versions.

Play link

Provide coloured play dough, card, coloured pens, scissors and 'goggly' eyes. Encourage the children to experiment in making their own scary monsters from the dough and adding extra features drawn onto and shaped from card. **(CD)**

Home link

Display the photographs of the monster's adventures and the play dough models to encourage the children to tell their parents or carers about their monster stories.

Cross-curricular links

Exploring Media and Materials
● Create constructions, collages, painting and drawings. **(CD)**

Early Learning Goals
● Explore colour, texture, shape, form and space in two or three dimensions. **(CD)**

A windy day

This activity encourages the children to ask questions and give explanations about why things happen when they experience the effects and sounds of the wind.

What you need
Balloons; balloon pump; wool.

What to do
● Choose a very windy day. Go outside into a safe area and let the children enjoy running about in the wind, feeling it blowing against their faces and through their hair. Suggest that they either stand with arms outstretched, facing into the wind so that they can feel its force or run with the wind behind them.

● Encourage the children to look around for other signs that the wind is blowing, such as noticing tree branches bending, and leaves, washing or clouds moving. Invite them to try to catch any leaves that are being blown along. Then gather the children together and ask: *How do you know*

it is windy? Can you see the wind? Can you hear it? Can you touch it? What is wind? Talk about the wind as moving air.

● Value the children's contributions and explanations and encourage them to listen to, and comment and develop on, what others have to say.

● Go back inside and show the children the balloons and balloon pump. Let them feel the air blowing as you demonstrate use of the pump. Start to blow up one of the balloons and invite the children to ask questions and comment on what is happening as the balloon gets bigger. Tell the children that, as you pump in more air, the balloon is stretching and getting bigger. Tie a length of wool firmly around the neck of

each balloon and ask the children what they think will happen if they take the balloons outside.

● Give each child a balloon to hold. Take the children outside, encouraging them to watch the balloons blowing in the wind and feel them pulling on the strings. You may decide to allow the children to let go of the balloons and watch them being blown away by the wind. Encourage them to speculate where they will land.

● Tie a bunch of balloons onto a fence or post that can be seen from inside the setting to encourage further talk and questions over the rest of the day.

Support and extension

● Support younger children by giving them extra time to think and put into words what they see, feel and experience when playing in the wind.

● Challenge older children to listen carefully and respond to other children's comments and explanations.

Further activities

● Make a collection of wind chimes and tie these to a tree or lines outside. Encourage the children to talk about how the sounds made by the chimes change, depending on

the materials they are made from and the strength of the wind. Encourage children to enjoy the sounds of words such as *tinkling, jingling, jangling, clinking* and *clattering*.

● Share stories on the themes of wind and balloons. These could include *The Wind Blew* by Pat Hutchins, *Elmer and the Wind* by David McKee, *Spot's Windy Day* by Eric Hill and *The Blue Balloon* by Mick Inkpen.

Play link

Provide a box of ribbons, windmills and 'floaty' scarves for children to enjoy playing with in the wind. Play alongside the children, encouraging them to talk about the ways in which the ribbons and scarves are blown about by the wind. Talk about why the windmills turn faster if held in certain directions. **(KUW)**

Home link

Suggest that parents and carers give their children time to enjoy experiencing and talking about the weather on the way to and from the setting and on other occasions when they are out and about.

Cross-curricular links
Exploration and Investigation
● Explain own knowledge and understanding, and ask appropriate questions of others. **(KUW)**
Early Learning Goal
● Ask questions about why things happen and how things work. **(KUW)**

Language for thinking

Holes and heaps

This garden activity gives the children plenty to talk and think about when they dig holes and notice the heaps of displaced soil getting bigger and bigger.

What you need
A wheelbarrow; a variety of spades, forks, trowels and spoons; watering cans and access to water; a safe, uncontaminated garden area or large containers filled with compost. Ensure that children are wearing protective clothing if the ground is damp and that they wash their hands thoroughly after the activity.

What to do
● Fill the wheelbarrow with the assorted spades, forks, trowels and spoons, and wheel it with the children to a garden area that is safe and easy for children to dig (or set up several large containers filled with compost). Ask the children what they think you want them to do with the equipment. If they do not suggest digging, ask them to choose one of the tools and start digging holes and piling the soil or compost into heaps next to the holes.

● Ask questions and make observations, to encourage the children to explain what they are doing and make connections between their ideas as they are working. Ask, for example:
● *Which spade do you think is best for digging a big hole? Why?*
● *What would you use to make a really small hole?*
● *The hole is getting bigger. Why is the heap of soil next to the hole getting bigger too?*
● *If you wanted a really big heap of*

soil, what could you do?

To answer this last question, children might suggest digging a bigger hole, putting all of their heaps of soil together to make one big heap or using the wheelbarrow to collect soil from another area. Encourage the children to talk about their ideas and listen to and develop each other's suggestions. Praise and discuss their suggestions and create an area together of holes and heaps of soil.

● Now gather the children together and ask them what would happen to the holes and heaps if it rained.

  ● *Where would the water go?*
  ● *Would it stay in the holes?*
  ● *Would it stay on top of the heaps?*
  ● *Could you use the watering cans to test your thoughts?*

● Supervise the children closely as they experiment in pouring water over the heaps of soil and into the holes, anticipating and talking about what they think will happen next. Encourage them to talk about their findings as well.

Support and extension

● Support younger children with the vocabulary they need to explain what is happening and to connect their ideas.
● Challenge older children to explain to another adult or group of children what they did, what they expected to happen and what they found out.

Further activities

● Develop the above experiment to prompt children further to talk about their ideas and anticipate what might happen. Suggest that they choose from various items, such as ice cubes, feathers (purchased from educational suppliers) and sand to put into the holes and onto the heaps. Ask: *Will the ice cubes/feathers/sand still be there tomorrow? If not, why not?*
● Provide a sand tray or sandpit of damp sand and ask the children to dig holes and make heaps of sand. Ask:

  ● *Is it easier to dig holes in the sand than in the soil? Does water stay in the holes?*
  ● *What happens to the heap of sand when you pour water onto it?*

Play link

Help the children to pat the surfaces of the heaps of soil and the insides of the holes until they are firm. Let the children use them as mountains and dips for 'off-road' toy vehicles to travel over. **(CD)**

Home link

Encourage the children to replicate the activity at home in the garden or on the balcony, showing their parents or carers what they have been doing and explaining what they found out.

Cross-curricular links
Exploration and Investigation
● Show understanding of cause/effect relations. **(KUW)**
Early Learning Goal
● Ask questions about why things happen and how things work. **(KUW)**

Mix a pancake

The children help to make real pancakes and enjoy tasting them before talking about and making their own from props in a role-play kitchen.

What you need
An A3 photocopy of 'The Pancake' on page 35; pancake recipe; pancake ingredients and orange and lemon juice; kitchen utensils needed to make and serve pancakes; cooker; role-play kitchen; role-play pancake ingredients such as sand, plastic eggs, water, play dough.

Early communicators begin to talk about and use objects representing the ingredients for their pancakes.
More confident communicators readily use and talk about objects used as symbols for other things in their role play.

Learning objectives
Language for Thinking
● Use talk to give new meanings to objects and actions, treating them as symbols for other things. **(CLL)**
Early Learning Goal
● Use language to imagine and recreate roles and experiences. **(CLL)**

What to do
● Teach the children the poem 'The Pancake' by Christina Rossetti with the appropriate actions. Ask the children if they have ever eaten pancakes and what they tasted like. Have they ever made them? Ask them to suggest the ingredients you need to make pancakes.
● Show the children the pancake ingredients, naming and talking about each item. Weigh the ingredients and involve the children in making the pancake batter together. Ask an adult to supervise the children, ensuring that they stay well away from the cooker, as they watch you cook and turn the pancakes. When cool, drizzle orange or lemon juice onto the pancakes, sprinkle with sugar and invite the children to taste and describe them. (Check that children do not have allergies or specific dietary requirements.)
● Tell the children that they are going to make pretend pancakes to share with their friends. Take them to the role-play kitchen area, explaining that they need to choose pretend ingredients, such as sand for sugar, and paper or play dough as pretend pancakes. Play alongside the children, encouraging them to talk about the items they are using.

Support and extension
● Support younger children who may not be used to treating objects as symbols for other things in their play.
● Challenge older children to explain what they are doing as they go along, including the symbolic items imaginatively in their play.

Further activities
● Re-read 'The Pancake' with accompanying actions. Encourage the children to use illustration cues when reading. Can they count how many times the word *pancake* appears in the poem?
● Talk about the tradition of making pancakes on Shrove Tuesday and having pancake races. Provide play dough and play frying pans for the children to make their own pancakes and hold races.

Home link
Suggest that parents or carers join in with their children's play, using representative items, such as a cardboard box as a cooker and shallow plastic bowl as a pan.

Cross-curricular links
Developing Imagination and Imaginative Play
● Use available resources to create props to support role play. **(CD)**
Early Learning Goal
● Use their imagination in art and design, music, dance, imaginative and role play. **(CD)**

The Pancake

Mix a pancake,
(Pouring flour into a bowl)

Stir a pancake,
(Stirring ingredients with spoon)

Pop it in the pan.
(Spooning mixture into frying pan)

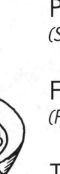

Fry the pancake,
(Pancake bubbling in pan)

Toss the pancake,
(Pancake being tossed)

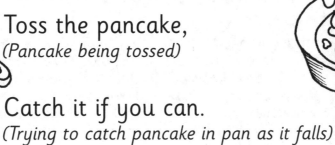

Catch it if you can.
(Trying to catch pancake in pan as it falls)

Christina Rossetti

Painting makes you think

In this activity, the children mix paints and create a giant abstract painting together, giving them lots of reasons to talk about and reflect on what they are doing as they work.

Early communicators begin to talk about and reflect on what they are doing.
More confident communicators begin to clarify their thoughts and comment on what they are doing.

What you need

A colourful stimulus (see What to do); powder paints; paint pots; water pots; thick paintbrushes; sponges; spoons; four sheets of A1 paper fastened together to form a big 'canvas', aprons.

What to do

● Choose one or more appealing and colourful stimuli, such as a bunch of flowers or flowering pot plant, a basket of fruit, a sheet of wrapping paper or a length of fabric. Vary this stimulus according to the season or to fit in with other themes you are covering.
● Show the children the item or items you have chosen and identify the colours. Prompt the children to notice that there is not just one red or one green, for example, but different shades of each colour.
● Tell the children that you want them to

help you use powder paints to mix pots of the colours they see. Ensure that the children are wearing protective aprons. As they mix the colours, encourage the children to talk about what they are doing and to come to decisions about any changes they need to make. Ask questions to encourage thinking and reflection:

● *Is this paint too thick? How can we make it thinner?*
● *I have some white paint. Can you help me make pink?*
● *What colour did you make when you put red into the blue?*
● When the paints are mixed, place the large piece of paper on the ground outside and invite the children to experiment freely in applying the paint to the paper. They could use thick brushes or

Learning objectives
Language for Thinking
● Talk activities through, reflecting on and modifying what they are doing. **(CLL)**
Early Learning Goal
● Use talk to organise, sequence and clarify thinking, ideas, feelings and events. **(CLL)**

sponges, or drip paint from spoons. Encourage them to talk about the effects they achieve and any changes they make. Prompt discussion through your questioning:
- *What happened when you dripped yellow paint onto the blue?*
- *Do you like using the brushes or sponges better? Why?*

Support and extension
- Talk through the steps of the activity with younger children.
- Help older children clarify their thoughts by reflecting on what they did and what they found out.

Further activities
- Provide a large sheet of cartridge paper and scissors, glue and a collection of collage materials such as textured papers, fabric scraps and wools. Invite the children to choose materials of the same colours as the paints they used in the main activity. They should create one large piece of art work together as they glue the materials to the paper. Work alongside the children, encouraging them to explain what they are doing, reflect on their work and modify it as they feel is necessary.

- Assemble a collection of rollers, inking trays, ready-mixed paints and a large sheet of cartridge paper. Let the children experiment in applying paint with the rollers. What do they observe as the colours mix together? Work with the children, modelling how to use the rollers, asking questions and making observations to encourage them to talk about what they are doing. When the work is complete, ask the children to compare it with their painting in the main activity, saying which they prefer and why.

Play link
Provide ready-mixed powder paints, palettes, water pots, brushes and paper to encourage children to experiment freely in mixing colours and to talk about what they are doing. **(CD)**

Home link
Suggest that parents or carers encourage their children to talk about and identify colours in the park, in the garden, in picture books or in their clothes.

Cross-curricular links
Exploring Media and Materials
- Explore what happens when they mix colours. **(CD)**

Early Learning Goal
- Explore colour, texture, shape, form and space in two or three dimensions. **(CD)**

New shoes

The children recall and share their experiences of buying new shoes. Then they listen to a poem and are inspired to take on the roles of sales assistants and customers in a shoe shop.

Early communicators are encouraged to talk about their experiences and use props in the role-play shoe shop.
More confident communicators recall occasions when they have visited shoe shops and build on their experiences as they take on key roles in the role-play shoe shop.

What you need

Photocopiable page 40; a suitable area in which to create a shop; tables and covered boxes on which to display shoes; laminated foot measure and *staff* and *customer* badges from page 41 (tape safety pins to the back of badges); toy till, purses, handbags, money; a selection of children's and adults' shoes for different occasions such as: slippers, novelty slippers, flip-flops, school shoes, ballet pumps, sports shoes, wellies and boots; card; felt-tipped pens.

What to do

● Ask the children to stand in a circle and look at each others' shoes. Talk about the shapes and colours. Discuss why we wear shoes and the different types of shoes needed for different occasions,

such as wellies, trainers, sandals or bridesmaids' shoes.
● Ask the children if they can remember and tell you about a visit to a shoe shop to buy new shoes. Talk through the process of buying shoes, including having your feet measured, deciding on the type of shoes you need, trying different pairs on and finally buying the shoes. Ask the children where else they could buy shoes.
● Tell the children that you know a poem about shoes. Read the poem 'Shoes', emphasising the jaunty rhythm of the words. Encourage the children to say and enjoy the sounds of lines such as:
  Scruffy shoes, shabby shoes,
  Shoes that shine.
and:
  Red shoes, blue shoes,
  Shoes that squeak.
● Ask the children to think about which shoes they

would have if they could choose any shoes at all. Show them some of the shoes you have collected and talk about when and where they might be worn.

● Explain to the children that you want them to help you set up a shoe shop. Display the shoes on boxes, set up a till area and make an *Open/Closed* sign. Make a simple model of a computerised foot-measuring machine using cardboard boxes: cut a hole in one box for the child to place his or her foot into, and add a dial made from another box to 'measure' the foot. Let children use the foot measure to 'measure' their own feet.

● Allocate the roles of sales assistants or customers and work alongside the children modelling the different roles as they are measured and fitted for new shoes.

Support and extension

● Support younger children in their talk by initiating and/or joining in with their role play.

● Extend older children's involvement by encouraging them to talk about what is happening and take on the character roles.

Further activities

● Create 'magic' shoes to sell in the shop. Provide plimsolls and glue, stars and

sequins and help the children to decorate the shoes. When they are dry, invite the children to choose a pair of magic shoes. What happens when they put them on? Do the shoes make them dance, run, hop or jump? Encourage the children to talk about the effects the shoes have on them.

● Using a large pair of men's wellies, help the children to paint the soles with a roller and make prints on paper. When dry, cut out the prints and place them around the setting. Share the story of 'Jack and the beanstalk' and follow the giant-sized footprints in the hope of finding the giant.

Play link

Take the play outside by setting up large shallow trays of different surfaces on which to try out different types of footwear. Use wellies in water, flip-flops in sand and boots in stones.
(KUW)

Home link

Ask children to compare shoes at home, looking for shoes that are bigger and smaller than their own.

Cross-curricular links
Developing Imagination and Imaginative Play

● Engage in imaginative play and role play based on own first-hand experiences. **(CD)**

Early Learning Goal

● Use their imagination in art and design, music, dance, imaginative and role play and stories. **(CD)**

Shoes

(Read to a beat, gradually increasing speed. Shout last line.)

Soft shoes, hard shoes
old shoes too.
Pumps, wellingtons,
a ballet shoe.

Trainers, slippers,
and flip-flops.
Shoes that jump and
shoes that hop.

Lace-ups, Velcro,
buckles galore.
School shoes, sandals,
clogs and more.

Walking boots, football boots
just like mine.
Scruffy shoes, shabby shoes,
shoes that shine.

Red shoes, blue shoes,
shoes that squeak.
Black shoes, brown shoes,
shoes that leak.

Your shoes, my shoes,
quite a few.
But, best of all
MY SHOES ARE NEW!

Brenda Williams

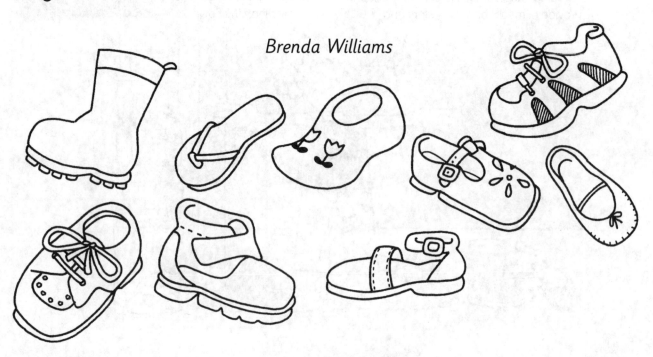

Speaking without hesitation

www.scholastic.co.uk

New shoes

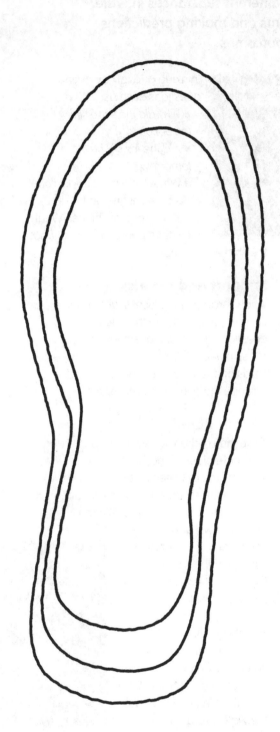

staff

staff

staff

customer

customer

customer

Speaking without hesitation

SCHOLASTIC
www.scholastic.co.uk

What will happen?

Children have fun with testing different substances in water, talking about their experiments and making predictions about the outcomes.

What you need
Large plastic containers; jugs; warm water; bubble bath; sand; food colouring; ice cubes; spent wooden matchsticks; page 43 photocopied onto card. Make sure the children are wearing waterproof aprons and are closely supervised throughout the activity.

What to do
● Examine and discuss the containers and other items collected. Explain to the children that they will be adding things to water to see what happens.

● Ask the children to pour warm water into a container and to predict what will happen if they add some bubble bath. They may expect it to make the water bubbly immediately. When it does not, ask them how to make the bubbles appear. Let them mix the water vigorously with their hands until the there are lots of bubbles.

● Repeat the process, adding sand, food colouring, ice and matchsticks to containers of water. Ensure that the children do not touch ice straight from the freezer. Encourage the children to predict what will happen, and to listen and respond to other children's ideas as they mix the substances in the water by hand. Prompt further

Early communicators begin to talk about what they are doing and make predictions about what will happen next.
More confident communicators clarify their ideas and thoughts through talking and explaining.

Learning objectives
Language for Thinking
● Begin to make patterns in their experience through linking cause and effect, sequencing, ordering and grouping. **(CLL)**
Early Learning Goal
● Use talk to organise, sequence and clarify thinking, ideas, feelings and events. **(CLL)**

thinking and talk by asking questions such as:
 ● *Why did the sand sink to the bottom?*
 ● *Will the ice still be there tomorrow?*
 ● *Why do the matchsticks float?*
● Ask the children to tell an adult or group of children what they have been doing and what they have found out.

Support and extension
● Talk through the process with younger children, encouraging them to ask questions and make observations.
● Ask older children to look at the sequence cards on photocopiable page 43 and arrange them in the correct order.

Further activity
Invite the children to use a dropper to add different-coloured marbling inks to a shallow tray of water. Point out that the ink stays on the surface. Draw swirly patterns in the ink with a stick. Ask the children what they think will happen if you lay a piece of paper on the surface of the water. Experiment in making more inky patterns.

Home link
Suggest that parents or carers encourage their children to add bubble bath at bath time and try to make the water extra bubbly.

Cross-curricular links
Exploration and Investigation
● Show curiosity about why things happen and how things work. **(KUW)**
Early Learning Goal
● Ask questions about why things happen and how things work. **(KUW)**

What will happen?

SCHOLASTIC

www.scholastic.co.uk

Not just boxes

When children discover an area full of large boxes and lengths of fabric, they are inspired to make their own creative choices and decisions about what the items represent and how to use them, talking and pretending as they play.

Early communicators are encouraged to create imaginary situations and use talk during their play, with the support of an adult.
More confident communicators initiate their own imaginary situations, creating and explaining their own scenarios.

What you need
A large clear area inside or outside; a selection of cardboard boxes; sheets, tablecloths and curtains; clothes airers; pegs; cushions; children's digital camera.

What to do
● Prepare an exciting scene before the children arrive in the setting. Fill the chosen area with cardboard boxes of assorted sizes, including some big enough for the children to get inside. Cover some of the boxes and clothes airers with drapes to create inviting tent-like spaces. Use pegs to fasten sheets together or to hold them back to create openings. Leave out a pile of cushions ready for use.

● Introduce the children to the area and give them time to play freely, climbing in and out of the boxes, exploring the area and developing their own creative ideas. Play alongside the children encouraging them to talk and become engrossed in their imaginative play. If necessary, make comments or ask questions to extend the play, for example:
  ● *I like your boat! Mind the waves – don't get wet!*
  ● *Let's hide under here. No one will find us!*
  ● *What's inside this dark, dark cave?*
  ● *Is that rocket going to the Moon?*
● Check first that you have parental permission to take photographs of the children and then help the children

Learning objectives
Language for Thinking
● Begin to use talk to pretend imaginary situations. **(CLL)**
Early Learning Goal
● Use language to imagine and recreate roles and experiences. **(CLL)**

to take digital photographs of each other as they play.

● Afterwards, gather the children together and invite them to talk about what they have been doing and the ideas they had during their play. What did they make? Where did they go? What did they find? Show that you value their ideas, creativity and originality. After talking together, give children further time to continue or extend their play.

● Print and display the photographs or present them as an on-screen slide show. Invite the children to talk about what they were been doing or making.

Support and extension

● Support younger children by introducing an idea for them to build on. For example: *Let's make a den we can hide in!* or *We could fly away in this plane!*

● Extend the play for older children by challenging them to work together as a group to solve an open-ended problem, such as: *I want you to make a den big enough for you all to hide in!* or *Make tunnels to crawl through.*

Further activities

● Introduce a new type of stimulus to the area by providing prop boxes containing, for example, dressing up clothes for kings and queens, a set of animal masks and a

selection of torches. Encourage the children to discuss, negotiate and include the items in their imaginative play.

● Remove the drapes and props from the area. Add cardboard tubes, pieces of card and sticky tape. Invite the children to use the resources to create one structure together. Encourage them to initiate, explore and talk about their ideas, taking the activity in any direction they choose and agree on. The finished structure can be incorporated into the children's imaginative play, with simple props they have made or chosen themselves.

Play link

Provide a variety of small-world people and clean cartons, sticky tape, glue and pieces of fabric. Encourage the children to use their imaginations to make structures and props to use with the play people. **(CD)**

Home link

Invite parents and carers to look at the photographs of the children's play, illustrating the fact that simple, recycled and found items can be invaluable in enabling children to be imaginative and creative in their play.

> ### Cross-curricular links
> **Movement and Space**
> ● Construct with large materials such as cartons, fabric and planks. **(PD)**
> **Early Learning Goal**
> ● Show awareness of space, of themselves and of others. **(PD)**

I'll always love you

**After sharing the warm, sensitively written story, *No Matter What*
by Debi Gliori, the children begin to explore and share their
feelings, including their love for family and friends.**

Early communicators begin to talk about what happened in the story and their own experiences and feelings. **More confident communicators** use talk to make sense of their feelings, relating them to the feelings of the character, Small, in the story.

What you need
No Matter What by Debi Gliori (2001, Bloomsbury Publishing); if available, soft toys/props for the animals in the story: a large and a small fox, a bear, a bug and a crocodile.

What to do
● Show the children the book *No Matter What.* Look at the front cover, reading the title and author's name and talking about the illustration. Then read the story, enjoying the rhythmic, rhyming text together.
● Ask the children to tell you about the two main characters in the story. Large cares for Small, but no reference is made to the gender of either character. Use the story to generate talk about the important people in the children's lives. Who looks after them?

Who loves them? Deal sensitively with children's comments and emphasise that different children have different main carers who love and look after them.
● Show the group the toys representing the characters in the story. Ask children to look after these and hold them up when they are mentioned, as you read the story again. Ask how the characters are feeling at different points and link these situations to the children's own feelings:

● *When Small was feeling grumpy he messed up his room. Do you ever feel grumpy? What do you do?*
● *When Small said that no one loved him, what did Large say? Do you*

Learning objectives
Language for Thinking
● Begin to use talk instead of action to rehearse, reorder and reflect on past experience, linking significant events from own experience and from stories, paying attention to how events lead into one another. **(CLL)**
Early Learning Goal
● Use talk to organise, sequence and clarify thinking, ideas, feelings and events. **(CLL)**

ever feel like Small?

● Repeat key phrases from the story and the refrain, I'll always love you, no matter what. Emphasise that it did not matter what Small did, Large would always love Small.

Support and extension

● Use the props to encourage younger children to talk about the story and how the characters are feeling.
● Encourage older children to explore when and why they might feel grumpy and how they might feel better.

Further activities

● Focus on the end of the story where Large and Small are looking at the stars and Large says, 'Love like starlight never dies.' Prepare a bag of silver-backed stars about 10cm in diameter, and give each child a star to hold. Ask them to close their eyes and think of someone who is special to them. If they would like to, they can tell someone else the name of their special person. Then, either write the person's name on the child's star, or ask the children to write the names for themselves. Hang the stars from a coat hanger or piece of dowelling.

● Talk about the way that Large cared for Small: bringing his tea, giving him a bath, reading a bedtime story, mending his toy, tucking him into bed and cuddling him. Bearing in mind and being sensitive to children's particular situations, encourage them to talk about the ways their special carers look after them. Can they think of anything they could do to show that they love their special person, such as offering to help with chores or giving them a hug?

Play link

Set up a 'caring area' and play alongside the children. Include items such as baby dolls, food, clothes, beds, bath, toy animals and their young. Model caring for the babies and animals, inviting children to talk about their needs.

Home link

Before they go home, ask the children to think of one thing they can do to help a special person in their lives.

Cross-curricular links
Self-confidence and Self-esteem
● Express needs and feelings in appropriate ways. **(PSED)**
Early Learning Goal
● Respond to significant experiences, showing a range of feelings when appropriate. **(PSED)**

Messages and clues

Hide and seek

The children listen to the poem 'Octopus', from Giles Andreae's *Commotion in the Ocean*. Then they hear a recorded message from the mummy octopus and help her to find her babies.

What you need

Commotion in the Ocean by Giles Andreae (1999, Orchard Books); the octopuses from photocopiable page 49 copied onto A3 pink paper, cut out and laminated; blank audio tape and recorder; water tray with large stones.

What to do

● Before the children arrive, record a message on the tape, adapting it to suit the age of the children. For example: *Hello! I'm the mummy octopus in the poem. I have eight children and they are all playing hide and seek. Will you help me to find them?* Put the large octopus in the water tray and hide the baby octopuses behind or under the stones.

● Tell the children that you have just found the book and tape on the side of the water tray. Share the book with the children, looking through until you find the poem 'Octopus'. Compare the laminated mother octopus with the illustration in the book.

● Talk about the pictures and notice that each octopus has eight arms. Show the children how to 'hide' their thumbs and count their eight fingers. Re-read the poem and ask the children to join in by putting their thumbs together, palms down and wiggling their fingers like the octopus's arms and tickling their own tummies.

● Sit together in a circle and speculate about what might be recorded on the tape. Show the children how to press buttons to play the tape. Listen to the message and talk about what you need to do to help.

● When all of the baby octopuses are found, count them and reunite them with their mummy.

Support and extension

● Model attentive listening when younger children listen to the message on the tape.
● Challenge older children to choose hiding places for the baby octopuses and help them to record their own message saying where they are hidden.

Further activities

● Make up another story together about the baby octopuses getting lost and being found again.
● Provide pink paper, felt-tipped pens, glue and scissors for children to make their own octopuses.

Home link

Suggest that children play hide and seek at home, like the baby octopuses.

Early communicators are supported by an adult as they talk about their ideas and explain what is happening.
More confident communicators confidently use talk to connect their ideas and tell others what they think will happen next.

Learning objectives
Language for Communication
● Use language for an increasing range of purposes. **(CLL)**
Early Learning Goal
● Listen with enjoyment and respond to stories, songs and other music, rhymes and poems and make up their own stories, songs, rhymes and poems. **(CLL)**

Cross-curricular links
Numbers as Labels and for Counting
● Count an irregular arrangement of up to ten objects. **(PSRN)**
Early Learning Goal
● Count reliably up to ten everyday objects. **(PSRN)**

Hide and seek

SCHOLASTIC
www.scholastic.co.uk

Adventure!

The children look for clues in the contents of a backpack, work out that they will be going on an exciting adventure, and set off on a hunt for exotic wildlife.

What you need
Backpack containing magnifying glasses, binoculars, digital camera, notepad and pencil, apples, small rug, photocopiable page 51.

What to do
● Hold up the bag and explain that it holds lots of clues about what the children are going to do. Invite them to take items out of the bag, name them and talk about their uses. Read the *Look out for…* text together and talk about the pictures. Ask the children why they might need the things in the bag and what they could do with them. Elicit the response that you could use them on an adventure.

● Set off outside together, taking the bag with you. Create the scene for the adventure as you go along, looking out for real and imaginary animals and features, including those shown on the sheet. Immerse yourselves in the adventure, stopping to listen for the sounds of birds and animals (real or imaginary) and talking about what will happen next.

● Examine leaves, tree trunks or insects using the magnifying glasses and look into the distance using the binoculars. Help the children to take photographs along the way.

● Ask them to choose a suitable spot for a rest. Sit together on the rug, eating apples and talking about what you have seen. Suggest that the children draw pictures or write notes in the notebook to refer to later.

Support and extension
● Model responses for younger children, including excitement, wonder and anticipation.

● Challenge older children to draw and talk about imaginary things that they saw on the adventure.

Further activities
● Ask the children to recount their adventure. Make a simple line drawing to show each event as the children mention it. Then help the children to arrange these drawings in sequence to make a simple storyboard.

● Provide backpacks and items such as torches, magnifying glasses, binoculars, notebooks, pencils and mugs so that children can pack their bags and set off on their own play adventures.

Home link
Ask parents and carers to develop their children's thinking and talking by playing *I wonder why…* on the way to and from the setting. For example: *I wonder why that man is climbing the ladder* or *I wonder why that baby is crying*.

Early communicators begin to talk about what they see and hear on their adventure.
More confident communicators become immersed in the adventure, expressing their ideas and feelings.

Learning objectives
Language for Thinking
● Use talk to connect ideas, explain what is happening and anticipate what might happen next. **(CLL)**
Early Learning Goal
● Use talk to organise, sequence and clarify thinking, ideas, feelings and events. **(CLL)**

Cross-curricular links
Dispositions and Attitudes
● Seek and delight in new experiences. **(PSED)**
Early Learning Goal
● Be confident to try new activities, initiate ideas and speak in a familiar group. **(PSED)**

50

Adventure!

Look out for...

monkeys

parrots

mountains

the river

the forest

a lake with fish

Guests for breakfast

Here, the children discover a table set for breakfast. Can they work out together which storybook characters will be visiting?

Early communicators begin to talk about familiar stories and their characters.
More confident communicators become involved in the imaginary worlds of stories, talking about the events and characters and making up their own stories.

What you need

A copy of 'Goldilocks and the Three Bears'; a table set for three using large, medium and small place mats, bowls, spoons and mugs; a packet of porridge oats; a milk jug; a container labelled *honey*; large, medium and small teddy bears; a doll.

What to do

● In the weeks before this activity, share traditional stories with the children, including 'Goldilocks and the Three Bears', so that they are familiar with the characters and storyline.
● Show the children the table. Elicit that it is set for breakfast and explain that you want them to work out who is coming for breakfast by looking for clues. Count the bowls, spoons, mugs and place mats and talk about the three different sizes.

Initiate thoughtful discussion:
   ● *How many visitors do you think are coming?*
   ● *Why are the bowls, spoons and mugs different sizes?*
   ● *What do you think they will be eating?*
   ● *What is the honey for?*
● Talk about the stories the children know, and decide together which characters they think would use the things on the table.
● When the children have worked out that the table is set for the three bears, share the story again, encouraging the children to join in with the repeated phrases. Ask the children to retell the story using the teddy bears and the doll, as props.

Learning objectives
Language for Communication
● Describe main story settings, events and principal characters. **(CLL)**
Early Learning Goal
● Listen with enjoyment, and respond to stories, songs and other music, rhymes and poems and make up their own stories, songs, rhymes and poems. **(CLL)**
Reading
● Listen to and join in with stories and poems, one-to-one and also in small groups. **(CLL)**
Early Learning Goal
● Retell narratives in correct sequence, drawing on language patterns of stories. **(CLL)**

● Later, when the children are out of the room, rearrange the table by putting a little porridge into the bowls and onto the spoons, spilling some milk on the table and laying a mug on its side to give the impression that the bears have been and eaten their breakfast. Build up the excitement when the children discover the scene, encouraging them to let their imaginations fill in the details of what must have happened.

Support and extension

● To help younger children understand the sequence of events, encourage them to act out the story as you read it.

● Challenge older children to continue the story by thinking about where Goldilocks went when she ran away.

Further activities

● Help the children to make simple stick puppets for the three bears and Goldilocks: draw the characters onto card, cut them out and tape them to lollipop sticks or pencils. Invite the children to use the puppets in their play, making up their own stories.

● Ask the children if they have ever tasted porridge. Show them the oats and ask them

what needs to happen to turn the oats into porridge. Make some porridge, ensuring that the children are kept at a safe distance during cooking. Tell the children to count how many children there are in the group and set the table accordingly, counting out the correct number of place mats, bowls and spoons. Serve the warm porridge topped with honey and fresh or dried fruit. Ask the children to describe the taste and texture and give their opinions. (Check that children do not have allergies or special dietary requirements.)

Play link

Set up a small table and chairs, three bears of different sizes, bowls, spoons, place mats, mugs, play food and play cooker so that the children can set the table and make meals for the bears. **(CD)**

Home link

Ask the children to bring in a teddy bear from home. Create a relaxed story area where children can go to read or tell stories to their bears.

> **Cross-curricular links**
> **Numbers as Labels and for Counting**
> ● Count an irregular arrangement of up to ten objects. **(PSRN)**
> **Early Learning Goal**
> ● Count reliably up to ten everyday objects. **(PSRN)**

In the jungle

The children search for clues in a jungle poster, trying to work out which picture book the poster is about.

What you need

Walking Through the Jungle by Julie Lacome (1995, Walker Books); an A3 copy of photocopiable page 55.

What to do

● In the week before this activity, read and talk about *Walking Through the Jungle*.

● Show the children the poster and explain that it holds clues about a story they have read recently. Find and identify the animals and prompt the children to think about the stories they know about jungle animals. When the story has been identified, read it again, inviting the children to join in.

● Enjoy saying the animal noises together. Help the children to hear the initial sounds in the words, and point out the alliteration in *trump trump*, *chitter chatter* and *snap snap*. Say the words *see* and *be* and ask the children to think of real or made-up words that rhyme with them. Write the words on a board and read them.

Support and extension

● Emphasise the initial sounds in words to help younger children hear the alliteration.

● Ask older children to think of other animal noises, listening for the initial sounds being repeated.

Early communicators become aware of rhyming words and the initial sounds in words. **More confident communicators** make up their own rhyming words and become aware of alliteration in animal sounds.

Learning objectives
Linking Sounds and Letters
● Show awareness of rhyme and alliteration. **(CLL)**
Early Learning Goal
● Hear and say sounds in words in the order in which they occur. **(CLL)**

Further activities

● Make an impromptu indoor or outdoor 'jungle' by draping play equipment with lengths of colourful fabric or sheets. Let the children pretend they are moving through the jungle like the boy in the story, looking for the animals as they walk, leap, run, swing and wade.

● Staple 28 pieces of A4 paper together (landscape) to make a *Jungle ABC* book. Label the pages with the letters of the alphabet. Invite the children to each choose a jungle animal, says its name and identify the initial sound in the word. Find the corresponding page together and ask the child to draw a picture of their chosen animal.

Play link

In your outdoor play area, provide jungle animal masks, if available, along with a giant-sized piece of paper, pots of ready-mixed powder paints and thick brushes so that the children can create a painting of their own jungle scene while they pretend to be the animals.

Home link

Ask the children to say the names of people at home and think of or invent rhyming words, For example, *Mummy yummy*, *Daddy caddy*, *Joshua woshua*, *Isabelle disabelle*.

Cross-curricular links
Movement and Space
● Experiment with different ways of moving. **(PD)**
Early Learning Goal
● Move with confidence, imagination and safety. **(PD)**

In the jungle

What do you see?

Speaking without hesitation

Smile!

**The children work as a group to piece together a jigsaw and
find clues about how to look after an important part of their body.
Use this activity when talking about keeping healthy and
cleaning your teeth.**

What you need
An A3 photocopy of page 57
with the jigsaw pieces cut out,
laminated and put in an
envelope with the word *Smile*
and a smiley face on it.

What to do
● Explain that the envelope
contains clues about looking
after an important part of the
body. Read the word *Smile* and ask the
children to give you a big smile and then
smile at a friend. Tell the
children that the smile is a
clue. Ask: *When your friend
smiles at you, what can
you see?*
● Open the envelope and
show the children the
pieces of jigsaw. Examine
the pieces and work out
together what routine they
show. Encourage the
children to talk about their
own teeth-cleaning routines and why they
think it is important to keep their teeth clean.
Be sensitive to the fact that family
expectations vary. Assemble the jigsaw
together, using positional language in
your conversation.

Support and extension
● Ask questions of younger children and
introduce new words.

> **Early communicators**
> use the pictures as clues
> and talk about what they
> are doing.
> **More confident
> communicators** use the
> pictures as a starting
> point for discussion,
> using a wide range of
> words to express
> themselves.

> **Learning objectives**
> **Language for
> Communication**
> ● Use a widening range
> of words to express or
> elaborate on ideas. **(CLL)**
> **Early Learning Goal**
> ● Interact with others,
> negotiating plans and
> activities and taking turns
> in conversation. **(CLL)**

● Let older children take turns
in talking about their routines,
and encourage the use of
positional language when
completing the jigsaw.

Further activities
● Talk about other ways to
keep clean and healthy, such
as washing our hands, having
a bath or shower, and washing
our hair. Discuss what we use to keep us
clean, such as soap, shower gel, bubble
bath and shampoo. Check that children do
not have allergies to these products before
providing a range designed for children's
use. Prepare a bowl of warm water for
washing hands and encourage the
children to smell and feel the texture of each
product, talking about their uses.
● Turn the water tray into a
bath for baby dolls. Place
towels, flannels, soap,
shampoo, bubble bath and
toothbrushes in the area.
Encourage the children to
care for the baby dolls and
make sure they are clean.

Home link
Invite parents and carers to
join you when you arrange
for a dentist to come and
talk to the children about
looking after their teeth.

> **Cross-curricular
> links**
> **Health and Bodily
> Awareness**
> ● Show awareness of a
> range of healthy
> practices with regard to
> eating, sleeping and
> hygiene. **(PD)**
> **Early Learning Goal**
> ● Recognise the
> importance of keeping
> healthy, and those things
> which contribute to this.
> **(PD)**

Smile!

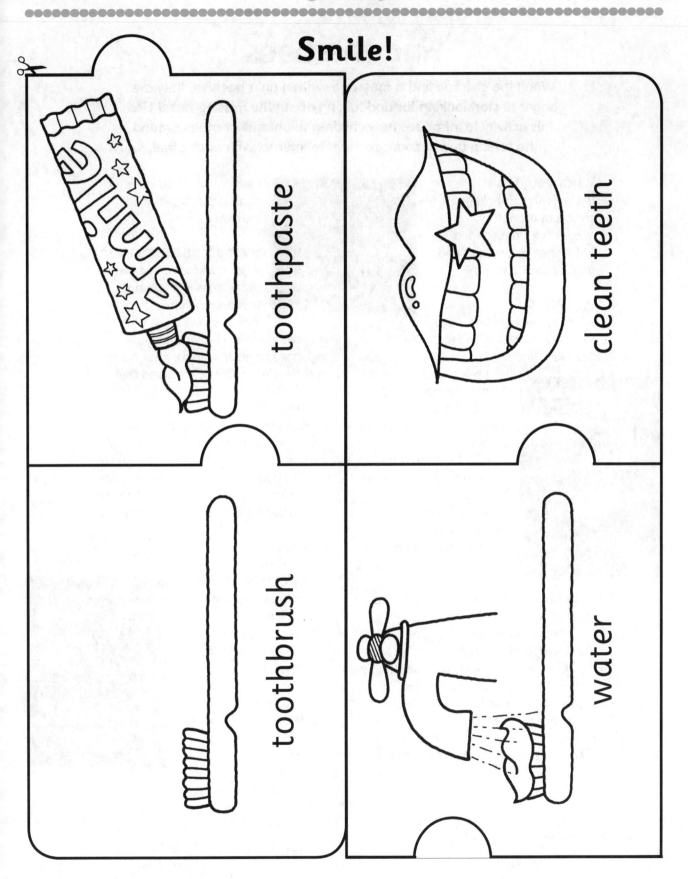

toothpaste

clean teeth

toothbrush

water

SCHOLASTIC
www.scholastic.co.uk

Find the bees

When the children find a message written on a beehive, they are eager to start looking for and talking about the missing bees! Use this activity to introduce new children to unfamiliar areas around the setting and encourage them to interact with each other.

What you need

The bees from an enlarged photocopy of page 59, coloured and laminated; a lidded shoe box; scissors and glue (for adult use).

What to do

● Tack the ten bees from page 59 around the setting for the children to find. Stand the shoe box on its end and glue the photocopied picture of the hive to the box lid. Cut a slit in the top of the box to enable the bees to return to the hive.

● Show the children the hive and read the message together:

Ten busy bees have buzzed away.
Can you find them all today?

● Ask questions to build up excitement and encourage the children to start talking:

● *What should we do?*
● *Where could we look?*
● *Do you think they have gone outside/ down the corridor/under the tables?*

● Encourage discussion and cooperation as you search high and low for the bees. Keep count of how many bees you find and how many more are still missing. When all the

Early communicators begin to talk about the bees and where they might be hiding.
More confident communicators talk together as a group as they search for the bees.

bees are found, count them again and return them to the hive.

Support and extension

● Ask questions and make suggestions to encourage younger children to talk as they search.

● Challenge older children to decide together as a group where to hide the bees and give clues about where to find them.

Further activity

Involve children in simple addition and subtraction activities, using some or all of the bees. Fix, say, five bees to a drawing of a flower and then ask one child to hide two of the bees. How many bees are left? If one bee buzzes back, how many will there be?

Home link

Teach the children this rhyme to share at home:

Here is the beehive.
(Clench fist)
Where are the bees?
Hiding inside where nobody sees.
Watch and see them come out of the hive,
One, two, three, four, five.
(Release fingers one at a time)

Learning objectives
Language for Communication
● Initiate conversation, attend to and take account of what others say. **(CLL)**
Early Learning Goal
● Interact with others, negotiating plans and activities and taking turns in conversation. **(CLL)**

Cross-curricular links
Calculating
● Show an interest in number problems. **(PSRN)**
Early Learning Goal
● In practical activities and discussion, begin to use the vocabulary involved in adding and subtracting. **(PSRN)**

Find the bees

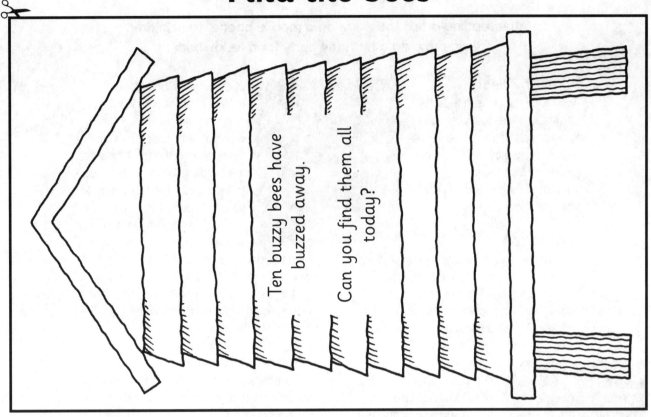

Ten buzzy bees have buzzed away.

Can you find them all today?

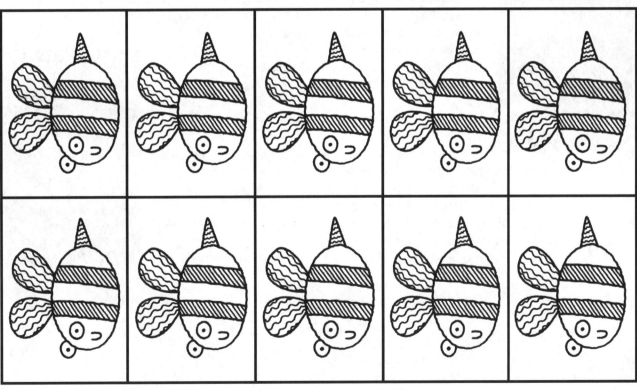

Speaking without hesitation

SCHOLASTIC
www.scholastic.co.uk

Ted is two today!

**After reading a text message on a mobile phone, the children
decide to plan a birthday party for a teddy bear.**

What you need

Two mobile phones; a teddy bear called Ted; soft toys; card; large sheets of paper; felt-tipped pens; play dough; role-play tea table; several laminated mobile phones from photocopiable page 61.

What to do

● Before you gather the group around you, arrange for an adult to send you a text message saying, *Ted is two today! Love from Tom*. Read and show the message to the children. Talk about the fact that it is a text message and must have been sent from another phone or computer. Speculate about who Tom might be and send a reply, pointing out the 'send' button.

● Suggest to the children that now you know it is Ted's birthday you could change your plans for the day and prepare a special treat for him and the other toys. Share ideas and list on the board things you will need: Ted, toys, treats… Read these words together and ask the children if they notice anything about the first sound in each word. Say the words together, stressing the *t* sound. Re-read the text message, listening for words beginning with *t*. Take

opportunities throughout the activity to point out the initial *t* sound in words.

● Make birthday cards with the number 2 on the front, and ask the children to write a message to Ted inside. Then ask them to search around the setting for a toy beginning with *t* to wrap up as a present for Ted. Make your own wrapping paper and tablecloth by writing the letter *t* in different coloured pens on large pieces of paper. Make party food using play dough, set the table and join the toys for the party.

Support and extension

● Collect items with *t* as their initial sound for children to touch and talk about.
● Challenge older children to touch ten items around the setting with *t* as their initial sound.

Further activity

Invite children to use whiteboard pens to write their own text messages on the laminated mobile phones and exchange the phones with friends.

Home link

Suggest that children look out for things beginning with *t* around the home.

Learning objectives
Linking Sounds and Letters
● Hear and say the initial sound in words and know which letters represent some of the sounds. **(CLL)**
Early Learning Goal
● Link sounds to letters, naming and sounding the letters of the alphabet. **(CLL)**

Cross-curricular links
ICT
● Know how to operate simple equipment. **(KUW)**
Early Learning Goal
● Find out about and identify the uses of everyday technology and use ICT and programmable toys to support their learning. **(KUW)**

Ted is two today!

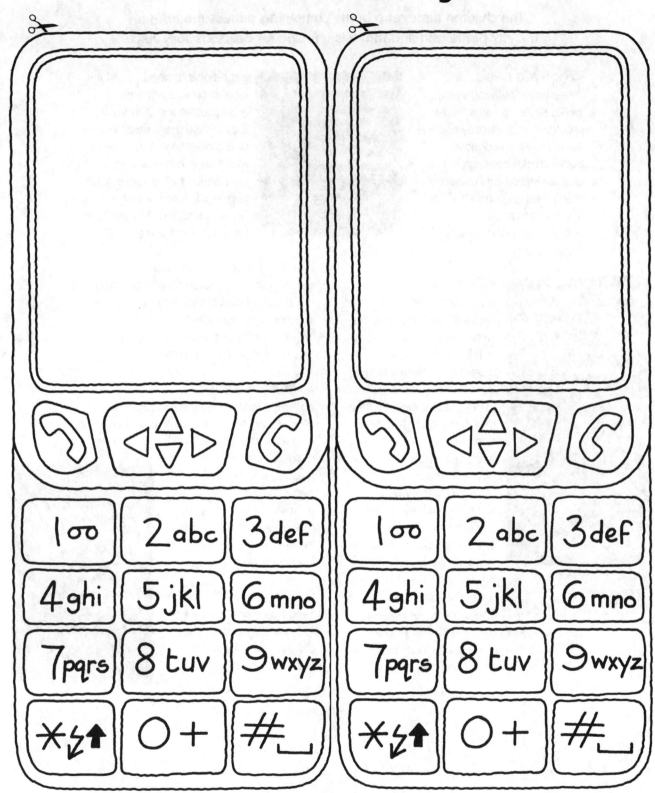

SCHOLASTIC
www.scholastic.co.uk

Message in a bottle

**The children discover a bottle containing a message from a
friendly pirate and find that it is a recipe for delicious Jolly Juice.**

What you need

Water tray containing sand, water, shells, toy underwater creatures; a photocopy of page 63; a wide-necked plastic bottle; pirate dressing up clothes; ingredients and tools mentioned on page 63. (Check that children do not have allergies or special dietary requirements.)

Early communicators pretend to be pirates and begin to hear and say some initial sounds in words.
More confident communicators role-play pirates and read the message with adult help, talking about the content.

Learning objectives
Language for Thinking

● Begin to use talk to pretend imaginary situations. **(CLL)**
Early Learning Goal
● Use language to imagine and recreate roles and experiences. **(CLL)**
Linking Sounds and Letters
● Hear and say the initial sound in words and know which letters represent some of the sounds. **(CLL)**
Early Learning Goal
● Hear and say sounds in words in the order in which they occur. **(CLL)**

What to do

● Put the pirate's letter into the bottle and float it on the water or hide it in the sand.
● Tell the children that today the water tray is just like the sea and leave them to discover the bottle. When they find it, open the letter and build up the excitement. Ask: *Who could have sent the message? How did it get here?*
● Ask the children to help you read the letter, hearing and saying initial sounds in words. Explain that a pirate has written down his secret recipe for Jolly Juice. Speculate about why he put the message in the bottle and threw it into the sea. Read the recipe together, using picture cues. Either conveniently have the

ingredients to hand or visit the local shop to buy them.
● Suggest to the children that they should dress up as pirates and make some Jolly Juice. Make sure the pirates wash their hands before making the juice drink. Find space on board a passing ship and enjoy tasting the Jolly Juice.

Support and extension

● Join in younger children's role play and talk about what is happening.
● Encourage older children to initiate ideas in the role play and to identify key words they recognise in the letter.

Further activities

● Provide coloured papers in different shapes and sizes, thick pencils and wide-necked plastic bottles. Ask the children to make their own pirate messages to put in the 'sea'.
● Provide a box of pirate dressing-up clothes and treasure in a treasure chest to encourage role play.

Home link

Send home photocopies of the pirate's recipe for the children to make with parents or carers.

Cross-curricular links
Developing Imagination and Imaginative Play
● Play alongside other children who are engaged in the same theme. **(CD)**
Early Learning Goal
● Use their imagination in art and design, music, dance, imaginative and role play and stories. **(CD)**

Message in a bottle

Ahoy there!

So you found our message!
Shhhh! This is the recipe for our favourite
drink – Jolly Juice. No one knows it but you.

1. Mix:
  1 cup of apple juice
  1 cup of orange juice
  1 cup of pineapple juice.

2. Add slices of apple.

3. Stir.

4. Drink the Jolly Juice!

Love from
the Jolly Pirates

Speaking without hesitation

In this series:

ISBN 978-0439-94499-1

ISBN 978-0439-94515-8

ISBN 978-0439-94556-1

ISBN 978-0439-94555-4

ISBN 978-0439-94558-5

ISBN 978-0439-94557-8

To find out more, call: 0845 603 9091
or visit our website www.scholastic.co.uk